World of Farming

Food From Farms

Nancy Dickmann

www.raintreepublishers.co.uk
Visit our website to find out
more information about
Raintree books.

To order:

☎ Phone 0845 6044371

🗎 Fax +44 (0) 1865 312263

✉ Email myorders@raintreepublishers.co.uk

Customers from outside the UK please telephone +44 1865 312262

Raintree is an imprint of Capstone Global Library Limited, a company
incorporated in England and Wales having its registered office at 7 Pilgrim
Street, London, EC4V 6LB – Registered company number: 6695582

Text © Capstone Global Library Limited 2011
First published in hardback in 2011
The moral rights of the proprietor have been asserted.

Edited by Siân Smith, Nancy Dickmann, and Rebecca Rissman
Designed by Joanna Hinton-Malivoire
Picture research by Mica Brancic
Production by Victoria Fitzgerald
Originated by Capstone Global Library Ltd
Colour reproduction by Dot Gradations Ltd, UK
Printed and bound in China by South China Printing Company Ltd

ISBN 978 0 431 19555 1
15 14 13 12 11 10
10 9 8 7 6 5 4 3 2 1

British Library Cataloguing in Publication Data
Dickmann, Nancy.
  Food from farms. -- (World of farming)
  1. Food crops--Pictorial works--Juvenile literature.
  2. Food animals--Pictorial works--Juvenile literature.
  I. Title II. Series
  633-dc22

Acknowledgements
We would like to thank the following for permission to reproduce
photographs: Photolibrary pp.**4** (Cultura/Bill Sykes), **5** (Hemis/Bertrand
Gardel), **6** (Index Stock Imagery/Inga Spence), **7** (imagebroker.net/
Martin Moxter), **8** (age fotostock/Emilio Ereza), **9** (imagebroker.net/Hans
Zaglitsch), **10** (Robert Harding Travel/Ken Gillham), **11** (Fresh Food Images/
Gerrit Buntrock), **12** (Index Stock Imagery/Lynn Stone), **13** (Novastock
Novastock), **14** (Hemis/Philippe Renault), **15** (LOOK-foto/Juergen Richter),
16 (Imagestate RM/Mark Henley), **17** (Johner RF/Johner Bildbyra), **18**
(White/Andrew Olney), **19** (Cuboimages/Alfio Garozzo), **20** (Glow Images),
21 (Stockbroker/Monkey Business Images Ltd), **22** (Johner RF/Johner
Bildbyra), **23 top** (LOOK-foto/Juergen Richter), **23 bottom** (Stockbroker/
Monkey Business Images Ltd).

Front cover photograph of a farm stand with an assortment of summer
fruits and vegetables reproduced with permission of iStockPhoto (© Jack
Puccio). Back cover photograph of a man hand milking a cow in Normandy,
France reproduced with permission of Photolibrary (Fresh Food Images/
Gerrit Buntrock).

The publisher would like to thank Dee Reid, Diana Bentley, and Nancy Harris
for their invaluable help with this book.

Every effort has been made to contact copyright holders of material
reproduced in this book. Any omissions will be rectified in subsequent
printings if notice is given to the publishers.

Contents

What is a farm?

A farm is a place where food is grown.

Farmers sell the food for people to eat.

Plants for food

peanuts

Farmers grow plants for us to eat.

Sweetcorn grows on a farm.

potatoes

Potatoes grow on a farm.

bananas

Fruit grows on a farm.

Animals for food

Farmers keep animals that give us food.

Beef and milk come from cows.

Bacon and ham come from pigs.

eggs

Meat and eggs come from chickens.

Getting food from farms

Farmers pick food when it is ready to eat.

The food is packed to keep it safe.

hot apple juice

Some farm food is made into other food.

wheat

bread

Wheat can be made into bread.

Oranges can be made into juice.

Milk can be made into cheese.

Lorries take the food to shops.

We buy food from the shops.

Can you remember?

What is bread made from?

Answer on page 24

Picture glossary

pack to put something into boxes. We pack food so that it is easier to move it from place to place.

shop place where we can buy things. Some shops sell food for us to eat.

Index

Answer to question on page 22: Bread is made from wheat. First wheat is ground up into flour. Then flour is used to make bread.

Notes to parents and teachers

Before reading

Ask the children if they have ever visited a farm. Ask them what food they think grows on farms. Make a list together. Can they tell you which foods are fruit, vegetables, meat, or grains? Explain that there are farms all over the world. Farms in different places can grow different types of food. Encourage the children to think about types of food that may come from other countries and how this food gets to them. For example bananas (shown on page 9) being grown in hot countries and being transported on aeroplanes and lorries.

After reading

- Get the children to brainstorm all the different types of fruit they can think of. Ask the children if they know what fruit grows in their country. Do they know where the other fruit grows? Do bananas grow where they live? If not, do they know why? Look at a map and talk about where in the world different fruit grows. Talk about how some fruit has to travel a long way for many people to eat it.

- Ask the children if they know what flour is made from. Show them some wheat stalks and some grains of wheat and explain how grains are ground to make flour. See how many foods they can think of that need flour. They could do a survey to see which of these foods each class member likes best and then make a tally chart together. Show the children how to make one of these foods, for example, bread, cakes, or pancakes.

24